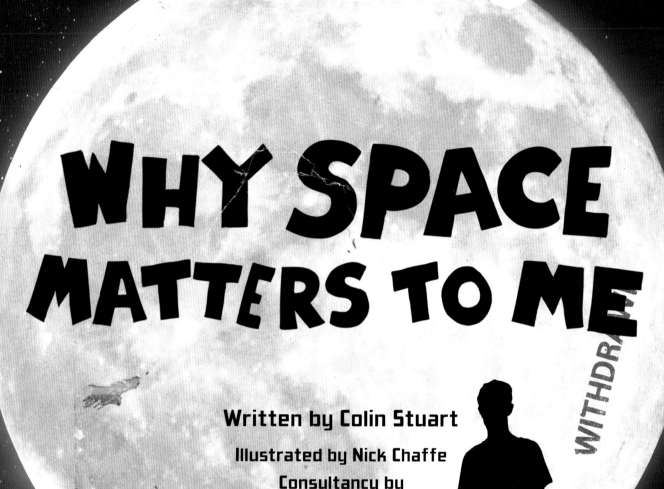

WHY SPACE MATTERS TO ME

WITHDRAWN

Written by Colin Stuart

Illustrated by Nick Chaffe

Consultancy by
Dr Jacqueline Mitton

RED SHED

EGMONT

CONTENTS

WHY DOES SPACE MATTER TO ME?

WE ARE MADE OF STARDUST

Your body is made up of lots of different types of atoms — mostly oxygen and carbon, but there are also others, such as calcium in your bones and iron in your blood. Soon after the universe began, the only types of atoms that it contained were hydrogen and helium. The rest were made inside ageing and dying stars. So, if most of the ingredients that make up you were made inside stars, how did they end up inside your body?

1 COSMIC KABOOM!

Big stars die with a bang. They erupt in a monumental explosion called a supernova — the universe's spectacular firework display that shines brighter than a billion stars. The force of a supernova explosion flings the oxygen, carbon, calcium, iron and other atoms far and wide into space.

This cloud of gas, called the Crab Nebula, was created by a supernova that exploded in 1054. The explosion was so bright that Chinese astronomers could even see it in daylight.

2 MIXING UP ATOMS

As the scattered atoms spread across the universe, they mix with the universe's hydrogen and helium. These cosmic mixing bowls are called molecular clouds.

The Horsehead Nebula is a molecular cloud. It is so tall that it would take our fastest rocket 100,000 years to cross it.

3 COLLAPSING CLOUDS

Our own star, the Sun, was born when gravity caused a molecular cloud to collapse. This happened over millions of years, and as the molecular cloud shrank, lots of clumps formed. The clumps got smaller and smaller until they became stars, one of which was the Sun. Some of the oxygen, carbon, iron and other atoms from the original cloud ended up inside the Sun.

4 THE EARTH WAS BORN

Some of the atoms formed a disk of gas and dust around the Sun. Over time, gravity pulled the grains of dust together to make clumps. These clumps collided with other clumps until rocky Earth and the other planets in our solar system formed.

YOU ARE 90.5% STARDUST!

Most stars look white at first glance, but they are different colours. The hottest stars shine blue.

5 AND THEN THERE WAS YOU

Over time, water broke down bits of Earth's rocks and some atoms ended up in soil. The soil fertilized plants, helping them to grow. When an animal ate the plants, some of the atoms became part of the animal. So, today, when you eat plants and animals, some of the atoms are passed on to you. But way, way before that, those atoms were made by old and dying stars. So you really are made of stardust!

9

WHY DO WE NEED THE SUN?

Without the Sun, all life on Earth could not survive. Plants soak up sunlight using their leaves in a process called photosynthesis. The plants turn carbon dioxide and water into sugar and oxygen to make food for themselves. They also provide food for animals and make oxygen for us to breathe. And millions of years after ancient plants died, they provide the fossil fuels that we use to power our cars and keep ourselves warm.

FOOD CHAINS

When animals eat plants, the energy in the plant is transferred to them. We can then get that energy by eating animal products, such as meat, fish, milk or cheese, or directly by eating the plants ourselves. This transfer of energy is called a food chain because energy moves from one living thing to another. All food chains start with the Sun.

Microscopic algae are at the base of this particular food chain in our oceans. To grow, algae need sunlight, water at just the right temperature and carbon dioxide.

At the next feeding level are the copepods, tiny creatures found everywhere in the oceans. These small crustaceans love nothing better than to munch on algae.

FOSSIL FUELS

When we use petrol and electricity, we are unlocking the power of the Sun. That's because they are fossil fuels, made from ancient dead plants and animals. When we burn these fuels, such as coal, oil and natural gas, we are unlocking the energy that those living things once absorbed from the Sun.

Hundreds of millions of years ago, long before the dinosaurs, the land was covered with lush forests and ancient swamps. The oceans were full of tiny organisms called protoplankton.

When the plants and creatures died, some of them sank to the bottom of the sweltering swamps and vast oceans. Over time, their remains were crushed by many layers of rock and water.

Peat

Lignite

Coal

Changes in temperature and pressure formed different fossil fuels. To make coal, plants in swamps first became peat. With increased pressure and a rise in temperature, this changed to a kind of coal called lignite. Over time, the lignite then changed to black coal.

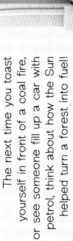

Today, we mine for coal, and pump out oil and natural gas from inside the layers of rock. The fossil fuels are then processed so that we can use them. They are non-renewable, however. Once we have used them, they are gone forever.

The next time you toast yourself in front of a coal fire, or see someone fill up a car with petrol, think about how the Sun helped turn a forest into fuel!

Solar energy

Fossil fuels will eventually run out and using them adds to global warming. However, we can use sunlight to produce cleaner energy by copying plants. Solar panels soak up sunlight just like the leaves of a plant. Rather than being turned into sugar, the energy is turned into electricity to power our homes, computers and televisions.

Mackerel are quick swimmers. In the warm summer months, they swim in large schools near the surface, hunting for copepods and fish larvae.

Small fish are eaten by large fish or other predators in the food chain. The Atlantic bluefin tuna can weigh up to 450kg. It is even faster than the mackerel so has no trouble catching them to eat.

TUNA

The next time you eat tuna, think about the food chain and how it all began with the Sun!

HOW DOES SPACE HELP US KEEP TIME?

What time is it? How old are you? How many months until your birthday? To answer these questions you need a way of measuring time. Our ancestors used space to keep track of time by using the Sun, Earth and Moon as the biggest clock of all. Today, our clocks and calendars still use their system.

EARTH IN A SPIN

You can't feel it but Earth is spinning on its axis. Day happens when the part of Earth you live on is facing the Sun. Night falls for you when the Earth turns you away from the Sun. Our planet rotates once in every 24 hours — once a day. We divide that time up into seconds, minutes and hours.

Earth

Axis

TELLING TIME BY THE MOON

We get the word month (or 'moonth') from the Moon. If you watch the Moon for a month, you will see its shape changes. This is because, as the Moon orbits Earth, it reflects different amounts of light towards us. We call these changing shapes 'phases', and you can see these phases below. It takes 29.5 days — roughly a month — for the phases to repeat.

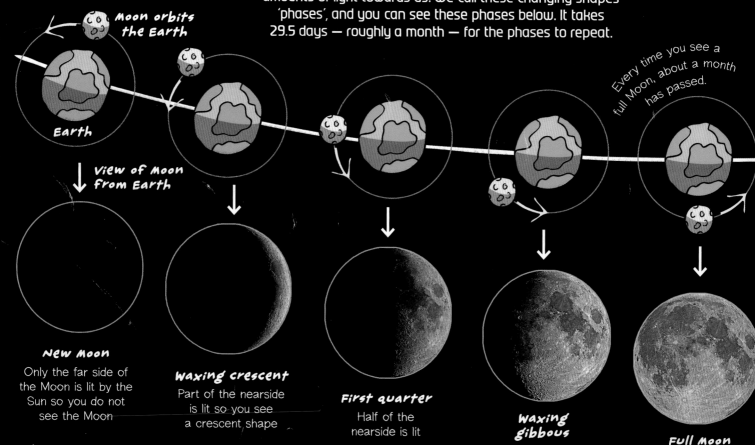

Moon orbits the Earth

Earth

View of Moon from Earth

Every time you see a full Moon, about a month has passed.

New Moon
Only the far side of the Moon is lit by the Sun so you do not see the Moon

Waxing crescent
Part of the nearside is lit so you see a crescent shape

First quarter
Half of the nearside is lit

Waxing gibbous
More than half of the nearside is lit

Full Moon
All of the nearside is lit

Sun

COUNTING BIRTHDAYS

How old are you? The answer doesn't just tell you how many birthdays you've had. It also tells you how many times you have been around the Sun. That's because a year is the time it takes for Earth – and you – to orbit around the Sun once.

Take a leap

Every four years there are 29 days in February, rather than 28. This is called a leap year and it is to keep our calendar matching what happens in space. It actually takes 365.25 days for Earth to orbit the Sun once, so we have three years of 365 days followed by one – the leap year – of 366.

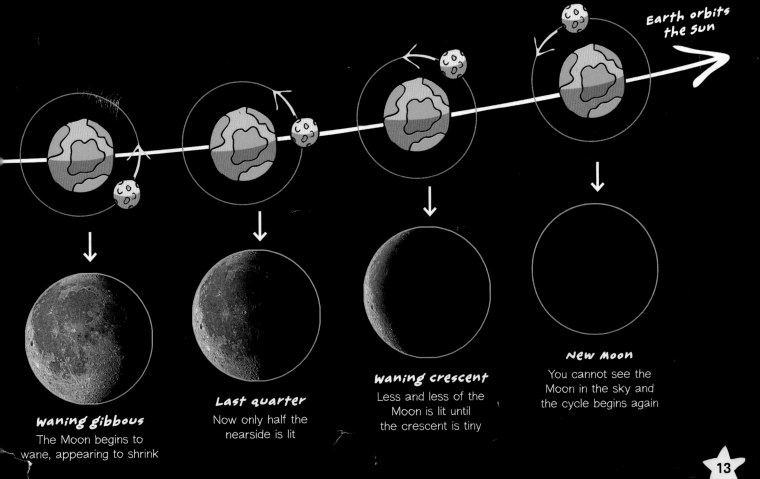

Earth orbits the Sun

waning gibbous
The Moon begins to wane, appearing to shrink

Last quarter
Now only half the nearside is lit

waning crescent
Less and less of the Moon is lit until the crescent is tiny

New Moon
You cannot see the Moon in the sky and the cycle begins again

WHY DO I GET COLD IN WINTER?

Throughout the year our planet changes. Summer brings long, sunny days; winter is dark and cold. Spring is the time to plant; autumn the time to harvest. The changing of the seasons affects the food we eat and the things we do. But why do things change in this way? It's all to do with the tilt of Earth.

SO WHAT CAUSES THE SEASONS?

The Earth spins on an imaginary line called an axis that runs from pole to pole. The axis is tipped over by 23.5 degrees. This means the Sun shines on different parts of the Earth at different angles during the year, causing the change in seasons.

June solstice

In June, the North Pole is pointing towards the Sun. This means that the Sun climbs higher in the sky in the Northern Hemisphere. There, the days are longer and the weather is warmer — it is summer. For people in the Southern Hemisphere it is winter.

Axis

Earth

IS IT WARMER NEARER THE SUN?

You may think that Earth is warmer in summer because our planet is closer to the Sun. But Earth is closest to the Sun in the first week of January when it is winter in the Northern Hemisphere. So the difference in distance is not the cause of our seasons and it is not warmer when part of Earth is nearer the Sun.

March equinox

By March, the poles are neither tipped towards nor away from the Sun. On this date the number of hours of daylight and darkness are exactly equal. It is spring in the Northern Hemisphere and autumn in the Southern Hemisphere.

NEVER-ENDING WINTER?

Can you imagine being plunged into a freezing cold winter that lasted a year, or being scorched by an intense summer that continued for many months? This does not happen because the tilt of the Earth's axis barely changes, and we have the Moon to thank for that. The Moon's gravity keeps us stable, stopping our axis from wobbling around very much.

Sun

December solstice

The North Pole is tipped away from the Sun in December. The Sun hangs low in the sky in the Northern Hemisphere, there are fewer hours of daylight and the weather is cold — it is winter here. In the Southern Hemisphere, the South Pole is pointing towards the Sun — it is summer here.

The word 'equinox' means 'equal night'.

September equinox

There is an equinox in September, with a day and night of equal length for both hemispheres. Autumn leaves are falling in the Northern Hemisphere; spring flowers are blooming in the Southern Hemisphere.

URANUS

Uranus is tilted right over on its side. This might be because something hit it or a moon pulled it over. It takes Uranus 84 years to orbit around the Sun so each pole has 42 years of constant darkness followed by 42 years of constant sunlight.

WHY ARE TIDES IMPORTANT TO ME?

The oceans of the world rise and fall as tides each day because of the gravitational pull of the Moon and the Sun, and because our planet is spinning. Using information about tides and the currents that they cause, we can safely swim, sail, fish and import many of the things that we use every day.

> We are able to sail small boats, canoe, swim and surf around many coastal areas. It is possible to do this safely because we understand how the tides and currents work and can avoid danger.

HIGH AND LOW TIDES

When the part of the world you are standing on is facing the Moon, water is pulled towards the Moon and the local sea level goes up — a high tide. The extra water comes from the sides of the Earth that are at right angles to the Moon at that time, so it is low tide in these two places. Water gets 'left behind' as a high tide on the other side of Earth because it is further away from the Moon and isn't being pulled as strongly.

Low tide

High tide because Moon's pull is weaker here

Moon

Earth

Water is pulled towards the Moon, creating a high tide

Direction of pull

Low tide

There are usually two high tides and two low tides every 24 hours and 50 minutes. As Earth spins, the Moon is also moving around the planet. This means that it takes Earth 50 minutes more to catch up.

The biggest difference between high tide and low tide occurs in the Bay of Fundy in Nova Scotia, Canada. The water can rise and fall by as much as 15m - the equivalent of three giraffes standing on top of one another!

Ships travelling from other countries bringing us cars, computers, clothes and toys can navigate shallow waters and arrive safely in harbour by understanding the tides.

Fish move with the tide to find food. Fishermen are able to catch them for us to eat because they know about the tides and where the fish are likely to be found.

Spring tides

The Sun is pulling on Earth's oceans as well, but because the Sun is further away its pull is only about half as strong as the Moon's. Twice a month, the Sun and Moon 'team up' and pull together in the same straight line. This makes the high tides particularly high and low tides particularly low. These tides are called spring tides.

Sun   Earth   Moon

Moon

Sun   Earth

Neap tides

When the Sun and Moon are both at right angles to the Earth, they aren't pulling together. In fact, they are fighting to pull the water in different directions. At these times, there are neap tides, when the difference between high and low tide is at its smallest.

WHERE DOES OUR WEATHER COME FROM?

Whether it is pouring with rain, the wind is whistling by or the Sun is beating down, the weather affects you every single day. It makes you choose to carry an umbrella, to walk or get a lift to school, or to play inside or out. Like many things on our planet, the story begins in space. Heat from the Sun is responsible for our weather and has a direct impact on the way we live our lives.

On 12 March 2006, 19-year-old Matt Suter was blown a record 398m by a tornado in southwest Missouri, USA, and survived!

Tornadoes can reach wind speeds of over 480km/h and travel more than 350km.

WINDY DAYS

Air moves because of a difference in air pressure, which is a measure of how much the air is pressing down on the Earth. Air gets lighter as the Sun heats it and the air pressure in that area decreases. Air from a place of high pressure rushes in to balance things out. The bigger the difference in pressure, the faster the air, or wind, is.

Clouding over

When the Sun warms the oceans, some of the water evaporates into the air as water vapour. The air becomes lighter as it is heated by the Sun and rises higher into the sky. But the higher it goes the colder it gets, so eventually the water vapour turns back into little water droplets that stick to tiny bits of dust in the sky. A cloud is formed when billions of these droplets come together.

If the water droplets in a cloud are spaced out, they let a lot of sunlight through and they seem white.

If the droplets are closer together, they block more sunlight and appear darker.

It never rains but it pours!

When water droplets first form, they are small and light enough to float in the cloud. Over time, the droplets gradually sink towards the bottom of the cloud and combine with other droplets to make bigger ones. When the droplets are too big and heavy, they fall out of the cloud as rain.

Let it snow

If the temperature of the cloud plummets below −10°C, it is cold enough for the water droplets to freeze around the tiny grains of dust. This results in snowflakes. The largest snowflakes happen when the droplets are tightly packed together in a cloud.

WEATHER ON OTHER PLANETS

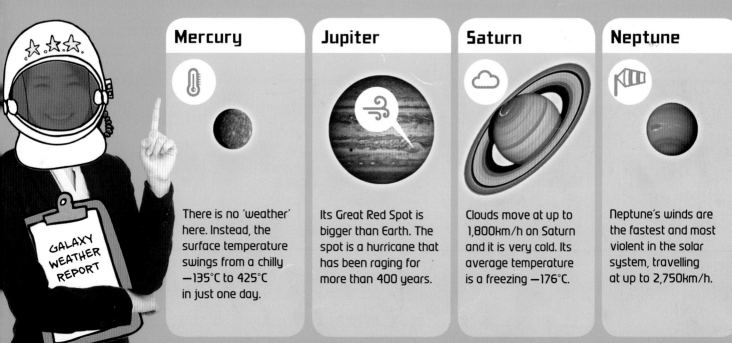

GALAXY WEATHER REPORT

Mercury

There is no 'weather' here. Instead, the surface temperature swings from a chilly −135°C to 425°C in just one day.

Jupiter

Its Great Red Spot is bigger than Earth. The spot is a hurricane that has been raging for more than 400 years.

Saturn

Clouds move at up to 1,800km/h on Saturn and it is very cold. Its average temperature is a freezing −176°C.

Neptune

Neptune's winds are the fastest and most violent in the solar system, travelling at up to 2,750km/h.

WHERE DOES THE WATER WE DRINK COME FROM?

Picture Earth without water. No wet stuff to sail on, swim in or drink. In fact, no humans or life at all. All life needs water, and water is all around us — 70 per cent of our planet is covered by the oceans. If you took Earth's water and placed it all on an area the size of Europe, the water level would stretch all the way into space! And that's exactly where it came from in the first place.

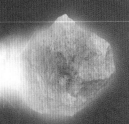

Scientists have used telescopes to investigate what asteroids and comets are made of, and have found that they both contain water.

BOMBARDMENT

When our planet first formed 4,560 million years ago, it was a seething ball of scorching magma — any water simply evaporated. Many scientists believe that the water on our planet was delivered by the asteroids and comets that relentlessly battered the planet in the Late Heavy Bombardment when Earth was about 500 million years old. During this time, our solar system was like a giant pinball machine with bits of rock and ice hurtling around everywhere, slamming into everything in their paths.

You can still see evidence of this battering today if you look at the Moon, which is covered with the scars of space rock impacts in the form of craters.

WHERE DID ASTEROIDS AND COMETS COME FROM?

The newborn Sun (see page 9) had a dark, dusty disk around it that contained some of the chemicals, including water, from the original molecular cloud. Over time, gravity pulled the gas and dust into clumps and some of them came together to form the planets. But there were bits of rubble left over that we now call asteroids and comets.

WHERE ARE THE ASTEROIDS TODAY?

There are asteroids all over the solar system. However, most asteroids are in a band between the orbits of Mars and Jupiter called the asteroid belt. Scientists believe that this area is home to between one and two million asteroids over 1km wide, as well as many smaller ones.

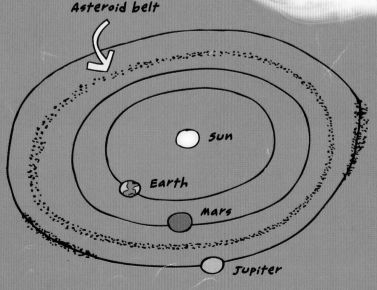

Asteroid belt

Sun

Earth

Mars

Jupiter

ARE ASTEROIDS DANGEROUS?

Travelling faster than a bullet, an asteroid the size of a large city races towards Earth. It smashes into the coast of Mexico. The impact sets off catastrophic events: violent earthquakes affect far-off lands and seas; a huge tidal wave climbs to the height of a 20-storey building; molten rock and boiling sea water shoot high into the sky; and fireballs rain onto the land as the entire planet burns! Could this happen? The answer is yes, it already has and it could happen again. . .

DEADLY DESTRUCTION

An earth-shattering event of this magnitude happened 65 million years ago. Travelling at 69,000km/h, an asteroid measuring 10-15km across smashed into the Yucatan Peninsula in Mexico. Seven out of ten of all living things on land became extinct, and in the seas, nine out of ten species perished. It was the end of the dinosaurs — the biggest creatures that have ever lived on Earth. Their extinction allowed mammals like us to inherit the planet.

When you see shooting stars in the night sky, you are watching bits of asteroids and comets burning up in the atmosphere!

The asteroid that destroyed the dinosaurs caused a global catastrophe – scoring 10 on the Torino Scale.

WHAT IS AN ASTEROID?

Asteroids are rocky or metallic objects that range from the size of a pebble to 950km across. Asteroids orbit the Sun, with 90 per cent of them in the asteroid belt (see page 21). They are debris left over from the formation of our solar system.

0	1	2	3	4	5	6	7	8	9	10
Virtually zero chance of impact	Impact extremely unlikely, worth monitoring	Close encounter with chance of local damage	Close encounter, 1% chance of local destruction	Close encounter, 1% chance of wide destruction	Close encounter, significant threat of destruction	Close encounter, possibility of global catastrophe	Close encounter, real threat of global catastrophe	Certain collision with local destruction	Certain collision with wide devastation	Certain collision causing global catastrophe

The danger posed by an asteroid or comet is measured on the Torino Scale.

Asteroid hit: February 2013
Where: Chelyabinsk, Russia
Size: 20m across – the height of a six-storey building
Torino Scale: 0
Speed: 69,000km/h
Frequency: Every 30-50 years

Asteroid hit: 50,000 years ago
Where: Arizona, USA
Size: 50m across – equivalent to the length of an Olympic swimming pool
Torino Scale: 8
Speed: 46,000km/h
Frequency: Every 1,000 years

SMALL BUT DEADLY

It's not only big asteroids that pose a threat. In 1908, a fireball about 50m across exploded in the air above Tunguska in Russia. It flattened 80 million trees and destroyed wildlife over 2,150km².

Asteroid hit: 2 billion years ago
Where: Vredefort, South Africa
Size: 5km across – the size of a small town
Torino Scale: 10
Speed: 150,000km/h
Frequency: Every 20 million years

IS THERE ANYTHING WE CAN DO?

The good news is that we are on the lookout for potential threats. NASA (see their Asteroid Watch on the web) are keeping an eye on all known asteroids and calculating if there is any chance of them hitting Earth within the next 100 years. If they do spot something, we will have a century to work out how to avoid a strike.

ASTEROIDS CAN MAKE YOU RICH!

There's more to asteroids than simply rock and water. Just one medium-sized asteroid may contain enough precious metals to make you a trillionaire! One asteroid in particular, 241 Germania, is estimated to be worth £56 trillion. That's roughly the same amount of money you get if you add up the yearly earnings of every single person on Earth.

WHAT'S IN AN ASTEROID?

You already know that our solar system was formed from a large collapsing molecular cloud (see page 9). That cloud contained heavier types of atoms, some of which ended up inside your body. Other atoms ended up in space rocks called asteroids. Asteroids contain precious elements such as gold, aluminium, platinum and palladium. Some of these elements are very rare and expensive on Earth. If we mine asteroids, this could bring down the price.

Platinum is used in jewellery and in some cancer-fighting drugs. However, its biggest use is in car exhausts, where it helps turn the engine's polluting gases into less harmful ones.

Palladium is found in things you use every single day: computers, smartphones, flatscreen TVs and tablets. And dentists use it to help rebuild teeth!

Gold is used in jewellery, electronic circuits, microchips and currency.

An asteroid just 1km across could contain 30 million tonnes of nickel, 1.5 million tonnes of cobalt and 7,500 tonnes of platinum.

Fuel station in space

One of the reasons space travel is so expensive is that you need powerful rockets to escape from Earth's gravity. Refuelling in space would make space travel much cheaper and might mean that one day humans will be able to explore the solar system more easily. Fuel from Earth could be stored on the asteroid, or it could actually be made there.

The water found in the asteroids themselves could be broken up into hydrogen and oxygen to be used as fuel to power any visiting spacecraft.

00.00
00.00

SO IS IT POSSIBLE?

Asteroid mining might sound like a crazy plan, but in 2005, a Japanese space probe called Hayabusa landed on an asteroid called Itokawa. The probe managed to collect around 1,500 tiny grains of asteroid dust and, in 2010, crashed back down into the Australian outback. Scientists retrieved the capsule and used the dust to learn more about the asteroid. This proved that it is possible to go to an asteroid and safely bring bits of it back to Earth!

Nickel is used in coins, stainless steel, armour-plating and batteries.

Iron is used in frames for skyscrapers, bridges, magnets and weapons.

Titanium is used in jet engines, ships, spacecraft, sports equipment and fireworks.

Cobalt is used in aircraft engine parts, blue glass, pottery and enamel.

Some asteroids are made of up to 80 per cent iron.

AM I IN DANGER FROM FALLING SPACE JUNK?

Earth is surrounded by a potentially deadly swarm that is growing bigger every year. This is no attack of killer alien insects; it's our rubbish. Broken satellites and bits of old rockets are just some of the millions of pieces of space junk that circle our Earth. Sometimes the junk falls from orbit. Larger objects — such as satellites — can come crashing to the ground, potentially putting you in danger. But smaller items, like the strange ones here, burn up in Earth's atmosphere.

TOOL BAG

Astronaut Heidemarie Stefanyshyn-Piper was fixing a solar panel on the International Space Station in 2008, when she let go of her tool bag. It spent eight months circling Earth and then burnt up in the atmosphere.

URINE

Everyone needs to go to the toilet, even astronauts! Sometimes their urine is ejected from the capsule. When it hits the icy conditions of space, it freezes into tiny crystals that orbit the Earth.

GOLF BALL

In November 2006, cosmonaut Mikhail Tyurin hit a golf ball while on a spacewalk. The ball orbited Earth for a few days before burning up in the atmosphere.

WHY DO OBJECTS FALL FROM ORBIT?

Objects fall from orbit when something — perhaps a collision with another object or friction with Earth's atmosphere — causes their speed to reduce. Picture this like a cyclist in a velodrome. Pedal fast enough and they are able to stay up on the high part of the track. Lose speed, however, and they will fall back down to the bottom, just as space junk sometimes falls to Earth. If an object can keep up enough speed, it will stay in orbit forever!

The amount of debris is likely to keep growing and collisions between objects break it into smaller pieces. Only by removing or destroying around ten large items a year can we stop this runaway scrapheap from piling up further.

COMING DOWN WITH A BANG!

One of the biggest satellites to return to Earth was Mir. It broke into large pieces that splashed into the South Pacific Ocean near New Zealand, in 2001. Large bits of space junk often end up in the oceans because sea covers 70 per cent of Earth's surface.

Space junk is monitored by scientists but they don't have much control over where the big objects land!

COULD I BE HIT?

You are more likely to be hit by lightning than space junk! So far, there have only been a handful of reports of people being hit by falling space junk. In 1997, American Lottie Williams was struck by a small piece of a falling rocket and, in 1969, five Japanese sailors were injured when junk fell onto their ship.

WHY ARE SOLAR STORMS IMPORTANT TO ME?

Schools close, trains can't run, flights are grounded, traffic jams snake around cities as everything is plunged into darkness. The cause? A solar storm! One of these sunbursts had exactly this effect on Canada in March 1989 and it could happen again — to you!

WHAT CAUSES A SOLAR STORM?

Magnetic forces twist and curl the gas inside the Sun and this churning can cause it to 'burp' out gas from its atmosphere — up to a billion tonnes in one go. Travelling at over 1.5 million km/h, these 'storms' surge out into the solar system.

SUN SPOTTING

Astronomers keep an eye on the Sun to see if a storm is coming in our direction. They use dedicated telescopes in space to watch the Sun 24 hours a day, seven days a week. The information sent back every day by just one of them — NASA's Solar Dynamics Observatory (SDO) — takes up the same amount of space on a computer as half a million music tracks!

DANGER FROM SPACE

A direct hit would cause massive problems — disruption of satellites, power lines, television signals, air travel and the internet. It might even kill. Without power there are no lights, phone lines or internet. Without phone or internet access, how can emergency services be contacted? Fortunately, most of the time solar storms miss Earth.

Activity on the Sun peaks every 11 years or so. During this 'solar maximum', Earth is more likely to be hit by a solar storm.

SPACE TECH ON EARTH

To explore space and understand a very different environment to that on Earth, scientists have to invent clever ways of solving complicated problems. Some of those ideas don't only help the scientists in their work, they have also been adapted to help us on Earth. Here are just 10 of these great inventions.

1. Memory foam

This temperature-sensitive material was first designed as safety padding for spacecraft and aeroplanes. Today, you can buy mattresses and pillows that, at room temperature, will mould themselves to the shape of your body in just a few minutes. Memory foam is also used in helmets worn by cyclists and for sports such as American football. The foam reduces shock if the wearer falls or is hit.

2. Artificial limbs

Lessons learned from work on robotic devices on spacecraft have been used to improve the design of artificial limbs.

3. Invisible braces

A tough material called TPA was invented by NASA to help track missiles. Its transparency and the fact that it is stronger than steel make it perfect for making 'invisible' braces to straighten teeth.

4. Baby milk

When researchers were experimenting with algae as a way of producing oxygen in space for astronauts to breathe, they found it contained some of the same chemicals as breast milk. These chemicals are now added to some artificial milks to feed babies on Earth.

5. Training shoes

Boots worn by astronauts on the Moon were specially cushioned because of the rough surface. The same technology is used in shoes worn for playing sport and running to improve shock absorption.

6. Forest fire alerts

In 2003, NASA developed software for use in satellites to scan Earth for potential forest fires. This automatic system gives people an early warning of the threat of fire. It helped to save lives in the 2007 Californian forest fire as well as many others since.

7. Scratch-resistant lenses

DLC (Diamond-Like Carbon) was first invented to keep astronauts' visors from becoming damaged. The scratch-resistant plastic is now found in the lenses of many glasses and sunglasses.

8. Jacket material

Mylar is a shiny material that is used to reflect heat from satellites. It is also used for jackets and ski parkas because its reflective qualities help to keep in body heat and provide a barrier from both cold and hot conditions.

9. Fire-resistant material

Modern firefighter suits are based on suits worn by astronauts. NASA worked with firefighters to develop fabric that was both heat and impact resistant, and a system to circulate cooling liquids inside the suits. They also installed infrared vision in helmets so that firefighters can work more efficiently because they are able to see where the hottest spots are in a fire.

10. Gel packs

These heat-absorbing packs are used a lot in spacewalks to transfer heat evenly around an astronaut's body. Today, they are also applied by athletes when they need to sooth sore muscles.

SATELLITES AND YOU

There are over 1,000 working satellites that zip around our planet, and chances are that you make use of them every single day without even realizing. Satellites beam hundreds of television channels to us, let us know whether it is likely to rain and help us find our way around. These machines moving far above our heads make an incredible difference to our everyday lives.

We can thank communications satellites for keeping us connected to the internet. Can you imagine having no access to the web?

Nearly two-thirds of satellites are used for communication.

Satellite TV wouldn't be possible without the hive of satellites that swarm around our planet.

The GPS satellite system has 32 satellites and there are always at least four of them above your head ready to exchange signals with your GPS device.

HIGH EARTH ORBIT
35,786KM ABOVE SEA LEVEL

Up here, in space, satellites take a day to orbit the planet. As the Earth also takes a day to spin, the satellites always stay above the same place on the ground. This is perfect for both communications and television satellites. If you have a satellite overhead all the time, your TV signal never gets interrupted.

Sputnik I was the first satellite to be launched. It was sent up by the USSR on 4 October 1957.

Sputnik I was the size of a beach ball (58cm wide).

MEDIUM EARTH ORBIT
20,350KM ABOVE SEA LEVEL

At this height, GPS (Global Positioning System) satellites orbit Earth twice a day. By sending signals to these satellites, you can work out exactly where you are on the ground. Animals, such as sharks and whales, can also be tagged with GPS devices to help scientists keep track of where they are going.

Voice-guided GPS systems in cars, called sat navs, and GPS trackers in smartphones help us to find our way around. It's really hard to get lost!

LOW EARTH ORBIT
160 TO 2,000KM ABOVE SEA LEVEL

Satellites in this orbit sweep around the planet in just 90 minutes. They include reconnaissance satellites used for spying, and satellites that monitor weather.

Spy satellites gather information for top secret missions – one could be spying on you right now!

Weather satellites can warn us about extreme weather, such as thunderstorms.

HOW CAN SPACE HELP ME FIND MY WAY?

These days, modern satellite technology means you can discover your exact location with the click of a button. But what if the satellites stop working? What if you were stranded in the middle of nowhere without any gadgets? You'd have to navigate the way people did hundreds of years ago. Luckily, space can still help you.

FOLLOW THE SUN

The Sun moves across our sky as the Earth spins. It rises roughly in the east before climbing to its highest point in the sky at around midday. Then it starts to sink back towards the ground before setting towards the west. If you need to head west to return home, for example, then all you have to do is follow the setting Sun. If you want to be more accurate, try shadow navigation to work out true north in the Northern Hemisphere or true south in the Southern Hemisphere.

Shadow navigation

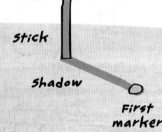

stick

shadow

First
marker

second
marker

No
(or s

1. Stand a stick that is approximately 1m long in cleared ground so that you can see its shadow. Then place a stone to mark the end of the shadow.

2. Now wait for 15 minutes. The shadow will move. Mark the end of the shadow with another stone. Find a straight piece of wood and use it to link the two markers.

3. With your back to the place your left foot again the first marker and you foot against the second. will now be facing true or true south.

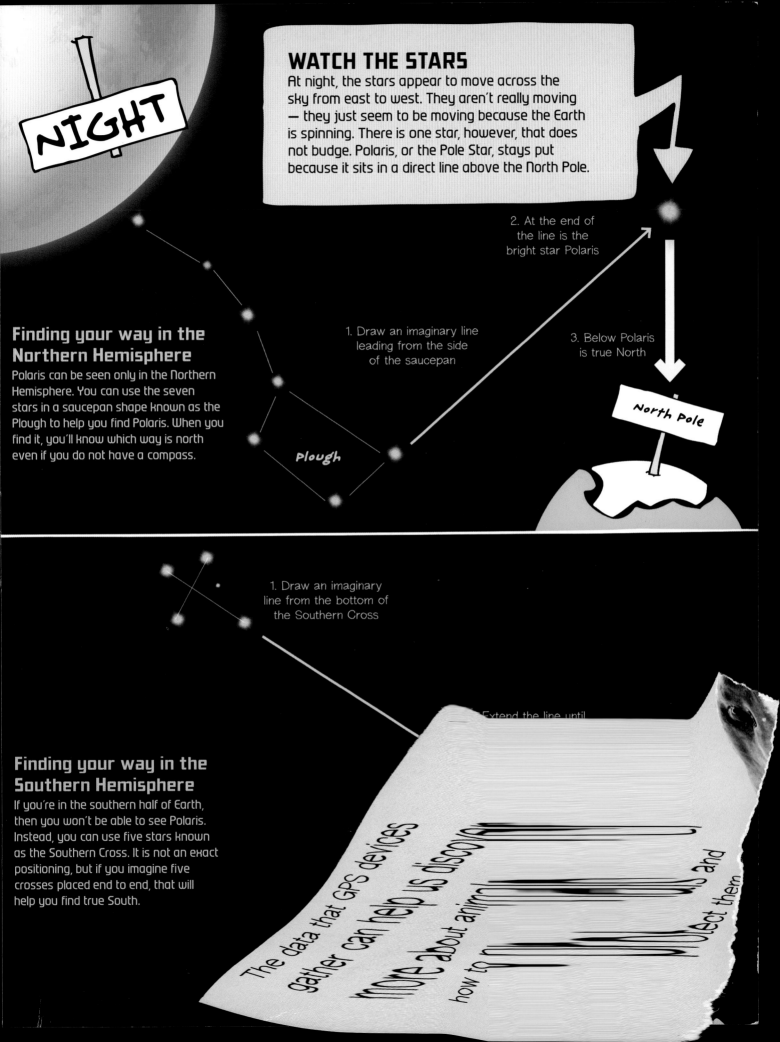

NIGHT

WATCH THE STARS

At night, the stars appear to move across the sky from east to west. They aren't really moving — they just seem to be moving because the Earth is spinning. There is one star, however, that does not budge. Polaris, or the Pole Star, stays put because it sits in a direct line above the North Pole.

2. At the end of the line is the bright star Polaris

1. Draw an imaginary line leading from the side of the saucepan

3. Below Polaris is true North

Finding your way in the Northern Hemisphere

Polaris can be seen only in the Northern Hemisphere. You can use the seven stars in a saucepan shape known as the Plough to help you find Polaris. When you find it, you'll know which way is north even if you do not have a compass.

Plough

North Pole

1. Draw an imaginary line from the bottom of the Southern Cross

Finding your way in the Southern Hemisphere

If you're in the southern half of Earth, then you won't be able to see Polaris. Instead, you can use five stars known as the Southern Cross. It is not an exact positioning, but if you imagine five crosses placed end to end, that will help you find true South.

Extend the line until

The data that GPS devices gather can help us discover more about animals and how to protect them

IS IT SAFE IN SPACE?

Humans have always dreamed of leaving Earth behind and exploring the universe, and by the 1950s we finally had the technology. But no one knew what effect going into space would have on the human body, so over the years they have launched many animal astronauts. The lessons learned from these intrepid travellers have made human space travel much safer.

ANIMAL EXPLORERS

To begin with, many different types of animals were sent into space simply to find out if they would survive. By analyzing how the different animals — particularly mammals — reacted, scientists were able to decide when to send the first men and women into space. Later, many different kinds of animals spent longer periods in space. This has provided insights into how we may be able to live in space colonies and travel safely to other planets in the future.

12 April 1961
Yuri Gagarin is not only the first human in space, he is also the first man and the first person to orbit Earth. From launch to landing the whole mission takes only 108 minutes.

31 January 1961
Ham the chimpanzee is trained to pull levers to feed himself with banana pellets to see if simple tasks can be done by a mammal in space. His trip, which is a test run, lasts just under 17 minutes. He performs his tasks successfully.

Ham

2 July 1959
Marfusha becomes the first rabbit to go to space on a USSR flight and return alive. She travels on a Soviet R2-A rocket with two dogs and went on to do many solo flights.

Earth

Laika

20 February 1947
Fruit flies are the first ever creatures to go into space. In the USSR. Their rough flight in just three minutes before being transported back to Earth alive.

3 November 1957
A stray dog from Moscow called Laika becomes the first animal to orbit the Earth. She dies soon after reaching orbit. Other animals are sent into space after Laika and are brought back alive.

16 June 1963

Valentina Tereshkova is the first woman in space travelling on Vostok 6. She orbits Earth 48 times, spending nearly three days in space.

14 September 1968

Two tortoises spend four days in space, completing the first ever journey around the Moon. This shows that living things can survive a lunar voyage.

20 July 1969

Neil Armstrong is the first person to walk on the Moon, saying the immortal words: 'That's one small step for [a] man, one giant leap for mankind.' Previous missions with humans on board had only orbited around the Moon.

28 July 1973

Scientists want to see if animals are able to do the same things as on Earth. On the Skylab 3 mission, one of the spiders, Arabella, spins the first ever web in space, although the threads are thinner than on Earth.

26 October 2012

Thirty-two medaka fish are taken on board the ISS to live in the new Aquatic Habitat. Scientists want to know what, if any, effect microgravity has on bone growth. With this information, they hope to be able to treat health problems in humans on Earth.

Tardigrade, seen under a microscope

14 September 2007

Tardigrades prove that some animals can live outside the cocoon of a spaceship. Three thousand of these tiny creatures go into hibernation to survive the extremes of space. This helps us to better understand life on Earth and the potential for animal life on other worlds.

International Space Station

2 November 2000

The first astronauts arrive at the partly-built International Space Station (ISS). With this permanent base in space, the astronauts set to work with experiments that help us improve life down here on Earth (see pages 38–39).

THE ISS AND YOU

Today, humans have a permanent base in space — since November 2000, there has always been someone living on the International Space Station. Slightly smaller than a football pitch, the ISS orbits Earth at a dizzying 28,000km/h and takes just 92 minutes to complete a lap of the planet. Astronauts on board conduct experiments that help us understand the human body and our planet, as well as outer space.

You can even talk to the astronauts on board as they orbit overhead as part of the Amateur Radio on the International Space Station (ARISS) project.

ONBOARD LABORATORY

The ISS hosts up to six astronauts at a time and they are responsible for running the space station as well as carrying out experiments both inside and outside the ISS. The results of their work are used to develop technologies to explore space. Some developments, shown here, have made life better for people on Earth.

Robonaut II is a valuable extra member of the crew and helps with tasks both inside and outside the ISS.

The technology that created the robots on board is now being used to develop technology such as the robotic NeuroArm that operates on the brain with the accuracy of a neurosurgeon.

LIVING IN SPACE

The six astronauts on the ISS have to live and work on experiments in an environment that has no gravity. This means that the way they do normal things, such as eating and sleeping, is very different. If you go into space to work on the ISS, here are some of the things you will have to do . . .

Meet the other scientists

Work in the laboratory

Farmers use cameras on board to monitor data on crop growth on their land. The data helps them make decisions, for example about where to add fertilizer. By reacting more quickly to problems they are able to keep up the supply of food that you eat.

The same system that purifies water for the astronauts is being used in Mexico today. Because it is solar-powered, it can give families who live in remote areas clean water to drink, so that they do not get ill.

Scientists have used the weightless environment of the ISS to test out treatments for cancer on Earth. They have developed methods to get anti-tumour drugs to the right place in the body.

The ISS has been used to track ships crossing the oceans when the vessels are far from land. This means that we can identify crowded shipping areas or the location of a lost ship.

In 2013, an experiment was conducted on the ISS that helps toothpaste and laundry detergent last longer on Earth – and therefore cost less – by preventing them from clumping over time.

Go for a spacewalk

Eat floating food

Sleep tied to the wall

SPACE 2040

Until now, space has been a destination that only a lucky few could visit, but this is changing. Within a few decades, space will no longer be just a place for highly-trained astronauts — it will be a place for you too. During your lifetime, you are going to see huge advances in space travel and you could be a part of it. Where might you be in space by 2040?

WORKING ON THE MOON

If humans are ever going to explore our solar system properly, we need good bases from which to launch. The Moon offers the perfect place for an astronaut headquarters. It is close by and has weaker gravity than Earth, so you don't need as much rocket power to launch from its surface. Imagine seeing Earth rise above the lunar surface for the first time.

HOLIDAYS IN SPACE

Picture the view from the window. You can see stars above you and the surface of the Earth curving away as the cities and continents of the world drift silently beneath you. You've just checked into the first space hotel. Whizzing around the Earth every 90 minutes, you witness 16 sunsets and 16 sunrises every day. According to NASA, space hotels are feasible. However, building them is dependent on the development of suitable and inexpensive transport to carry people and materials into space.

Space hotels like this would give you an out-of-this-world experience!

40

In 2040, will you be a passenger or a member of the crew on a flight to the Moon or Mars?

SPACE TOURISM

We have already entered the age of space tourism. As far back as 2001, American Dennis Tito paid $20 million (£11.8 million) to spend a week aboard the International Space Station. Very soon, Virgin Galactic will launch the first trip to space for paying customers. A ticket currently costs $200,000 (£118,000), but the price is likely to drop significantly in the decades to come.

WALKING ON MARS

If NASA succeeds in its aims, then human footprints will appear in the red soil of Mars by 2035. If successful, the mission could see many more flights head for the Red Planet, which is the most Earth-like of all the planets in the solar system. The good news is that you're the perfect age to be considered for future Mars exploration. Your jobs would include searching the dusty Martian surface for signs of alien life forms.

SO YOU WANT TO BE AN ASTRONAUT?

There has never been a more exciting time to think about working on space-related projects or even travelling to, or living in, space. Not everyone becomes an astronaut, but there are lots of ways in which you can get involved in exploring our universe — just look at some of the different people who are involved already!

SATELLITE ENGINEER

SPACE SCIENTIST

ROCKET SCIENTIST

PLANETARY SCIENTIST

ASTRONOMER

ASTROPHYSICIST

ASTRONAUT

PILOT

THEORETICAL PHYSICIST

ASTROBIOLOGIST

TECHNICIAN

PROGRAMME ANALYST

IT PROJECT MANAGER

METEOROLOGIST

DOCTOR

AEROSPACE ENGINEER

PAYLOAD SPECIALIST

COMPUTER SCIENTIST

COSMOLOGIST

INSTRUMENT MAKER

SPACE CENTRE ADMINISTRATOR

BECOMING AN ASTRONAUT

If you have your heart set on becoming an astronaut, the first thing you need to know is that the competition is very stiff. However, if you tick these boxes, then there is absolutely no reason why you can't do it if you set your mind to it and work hard.

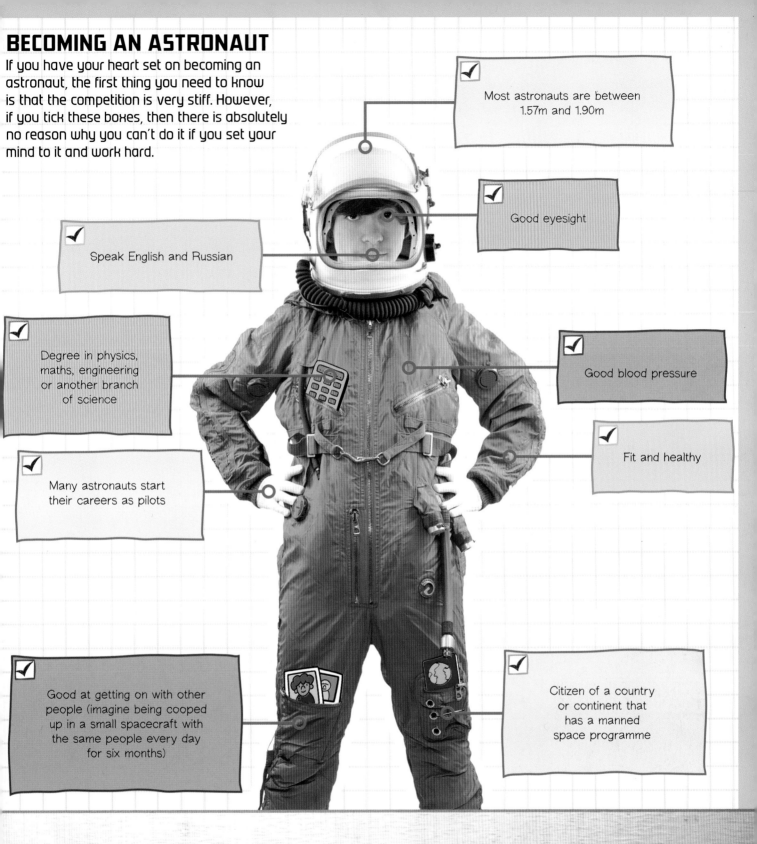

☑ Most astronauts are between 1.57m and 1.90m

☑ Good eyesight

☑ Speak English and Russian

☑ Degree in physics, maths, engineering or another branch of science

☑ Good blood pressure

☑ Many astronauts start their careers as pilots

☑ Fit and healthy

☑ Good at getting on with other people (imagine being cooped up in a small spacecraft with the same people every day for six months)

☑ Citizen of a country or continent that has a manned space programme

Where can I find out more about space?

- Take a guided tour of the International Space Station: www.youtube.com/watch?v=doN4t5NKW-k
- Find out all about space and technology: http://spaceplace.nasa.gov
- For asteroid news, go to Asteroid Watch: www.jpl.nasa.gov/asteroidwatch
- Learn about amateur radio contact with the ISS: www.nasa.gov/mission_pages/station/research/experiments/23.html

- Visit the European Space Agency: www.esa.int/esaKIDSen
- Explore astronomy, the solar system and modern space exploration: www.kidsastronomy.com
- Use this live portal to find out the latest space news: http://news.nationalgeographic.com/space
- Discover everything about astronauts and their voyages: www.bbc.co.uk/science/space/solarsystem/astronauts

GLOSSARY

air pressure
The way in which the layers of air press down on Earth. The greatest air pressure is found at ground level. The higher up you go, the less air there is and the lower the air pressure becomes.

asteroid
A chunk of rock and metal, left over from the birth of the solar system, that orbits the Sun.

astronaut
A person who has been into space. Russian astronauts are known as cosmonauts.

astronomer
A person who studies the stars and planets as well as other bodies in space.

atmosphere
The layer of gases that surround a planet or star. Earth's atmosphere is the air.

atom
A tiny particle of matter. Atoms are the smallest particles that can take part in a chemical reaction.

axis
An imaginary straight line from the top to the bottom of a spinning object, such as Earth. The object turns or rotates around the axis.

comet
A small chunk of ice and dust in orbit around the Sun. As a comet nears the Sun and gets warmer, gas and dust stream off its surface.

cosmonaut
See astronaut

crater
A bowl-shaped hollow in a planet's surface, often caused by the impact of an asteroid.

elements
The different basic materials from which everything we can see in the universe is made.

ESA
European Space Agency — an agency set up in 1975 by various European countries to explore space. Today, 20 countries belong to the ESA and its headquarters are in Paris, France.

food chain
A series of living things that depend on each other for food. A typical food chain starts with a plant that is eaten by a plant-eating animal. The plant-eating animal is then eaten by a meat-eating animal.

fossil fuel
Material that can be burned and comes from the remains of animals and plants that lived millions of years ago. Coal and oil are fossil fuels.

galaxy
A huge collection of stars, dust and gas held together by gravity. Our galaxy is called the Milky Way.

GPS
Global Positioning System — a global system of satellites that was developed to provide exact positions to help people travel by air, sea or land.

gravity
The force that pulls objects together. The gravity of the Sun keeps Earth in orbit. Gravity also makes objects fall and gives them weight.

hurricane
A violent tropical storm. Hurricanes blow at speeds of 120km/h or more.

microgravity
The very low gravity experienced in a spacecraft in Earth's orbit.

NASA
National Aeronautics and Space Administration — the space agency set up by the US government in 1958. It is responsible for the US space programme and undertaking space research.

Northern Hemisphere
The half of Earth between the North Pole and the Equator.

orbit
The path of a body, such as a moon or planet, around another body. Earth moves in orbit around the Sun.